APR   2016

SCIENCE OF SPORTS

THE SCIENCE OF FOOTBALL

with MAX AXIOM SUPER SCIENTIST

by Nikole Brooks Bethea

illustrated by Caio Cacau

Consultant:
Lyle A. Ford
Department Chair
Physics & Astronomy
University of Wisconsin, Eau Claire

CAPSTONE PRESS
a capstone imprint

Graphic Library is published by Capstone Press,
1710 Roe Crest Drive, North Mankato, Minnesota 56003
www.capstonepub.com

Library of Congress Cataloging-in-Publication Data
Bethea, Nikole Brooks.
The science of football with Max Axiom, super scientist / by Nikole B. Bethea.
pages cm. — (Graphic Library. The Science of Sports with Max Axiom.)
Includes bibliographical references and index.
Summary: "Uses graphic novel format to reveal the science at play behind the sport of
football"— Provided by publisher.
ISBN 978-1-4914-6085-6 (library binding)
ISBN 978-1-4914-6089-4 (paperback)
ISBN 978-1-4914-6093-1 (eBook PDF)
1. Football—Juvenile literature. 2. Sports sciences—Juvenile literature. 3. Graphic novels—
Juvenile literature. I. Title.
GV950.7.B46 2016
796.332—dc23   2015012517

Editor
Mandy Robbins

Designer
Ted Williams

Creative Director
Nathan Gassman

Media Researcher
Jo Miller

Production Specialist
Laura Manthe

Printed in the United States of America in North Mankato, Minnesota.
042015   008823CGF15

TABLE OF CONTENTS

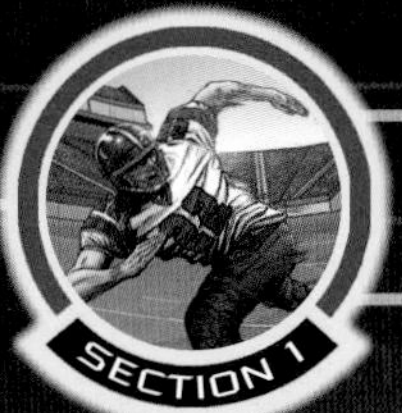
SECTION 1

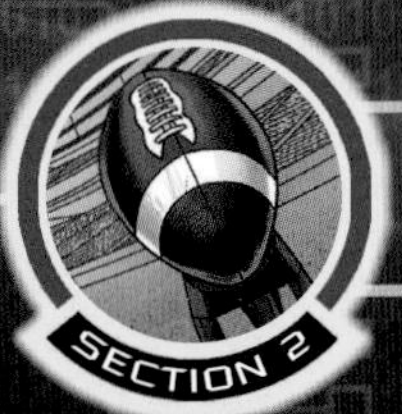
SECTION 2

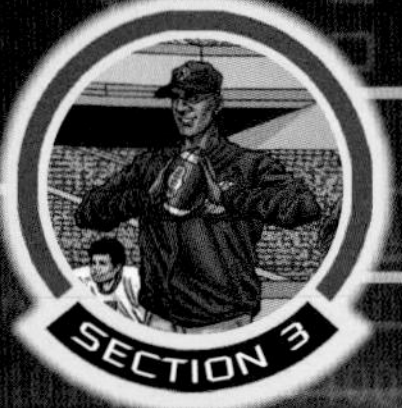
SECTION 3

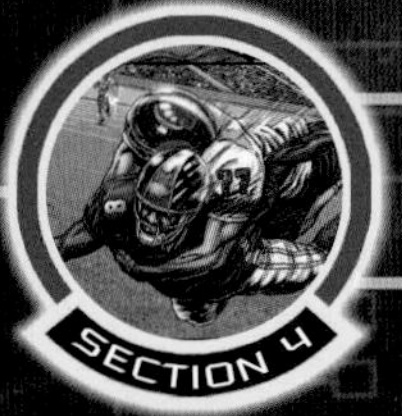
SECTION 4

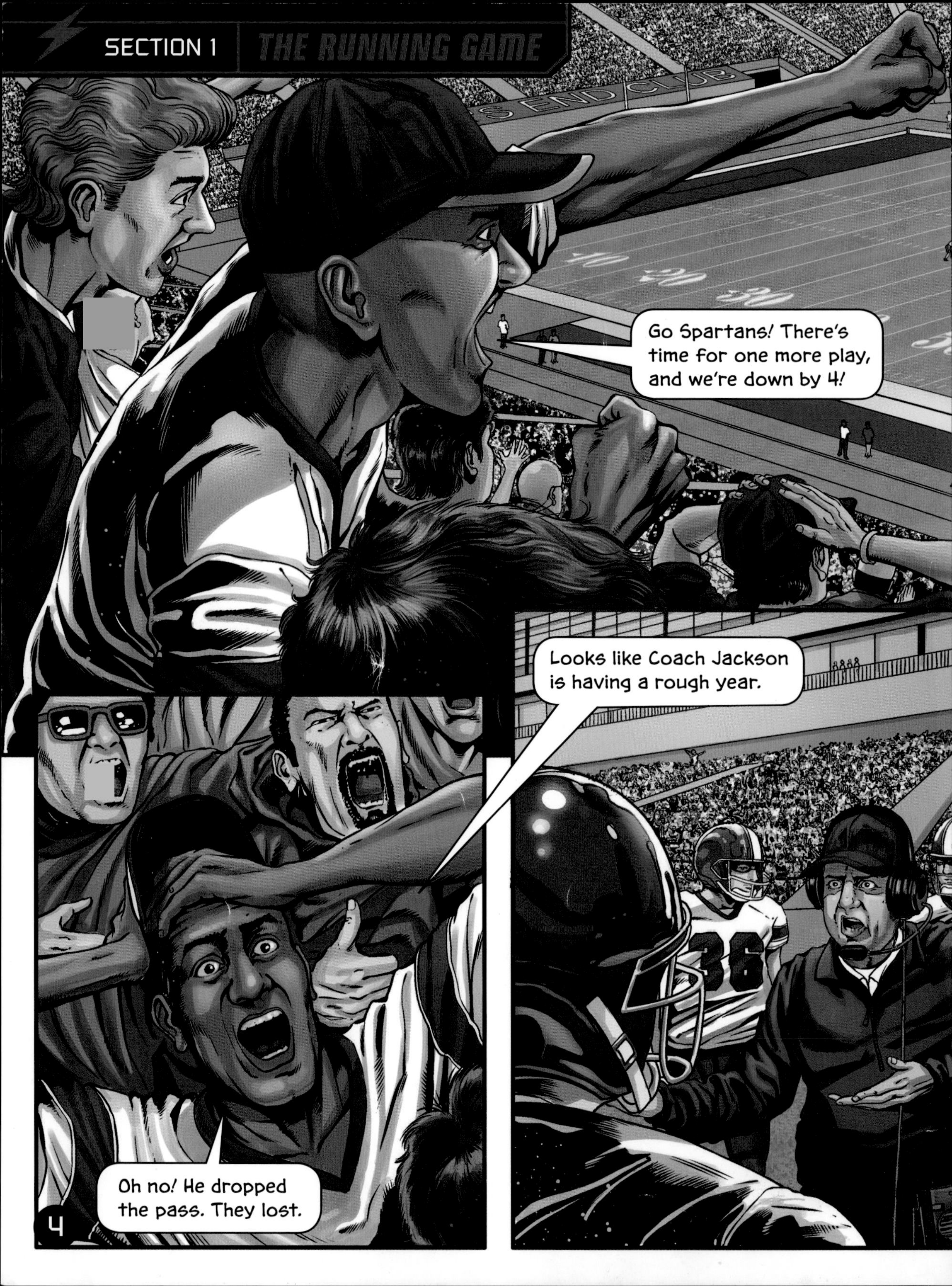
Go Spartans! There's time for one more play, and we're down by 4!
Oh no! He dropped the pass. They lost.
Looks like Coach Jackson is having a rough year.

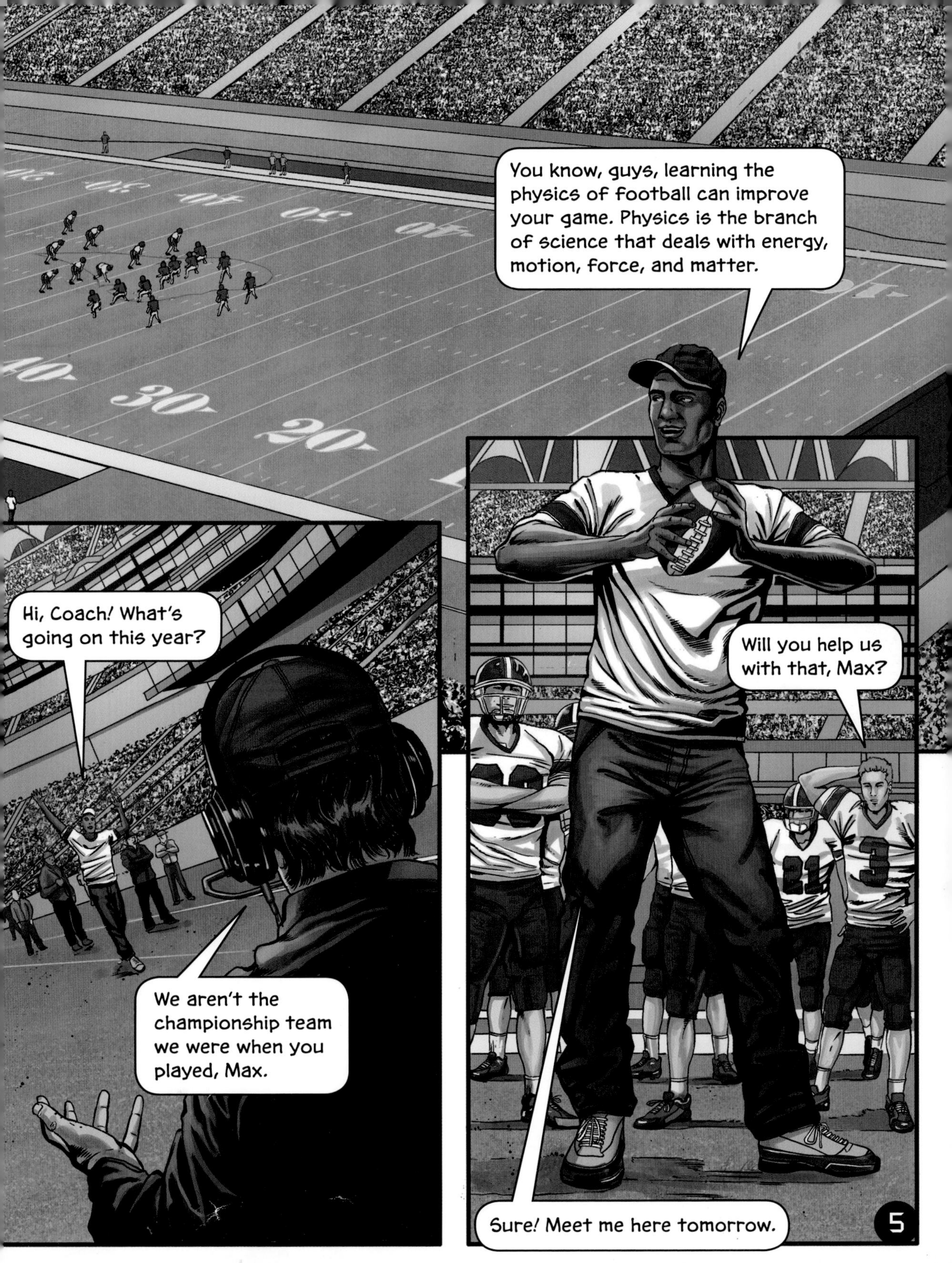
You know, guys, learning the physics of football can improve your game. Physics is the branch of science that deals with energy, motion, force, and matter.
Hi, Coach! What's going on this year?
We aren't the championship team we were when you played, Max.
Will you help us with that, Max?
Sure! Meet me here tomorrow.

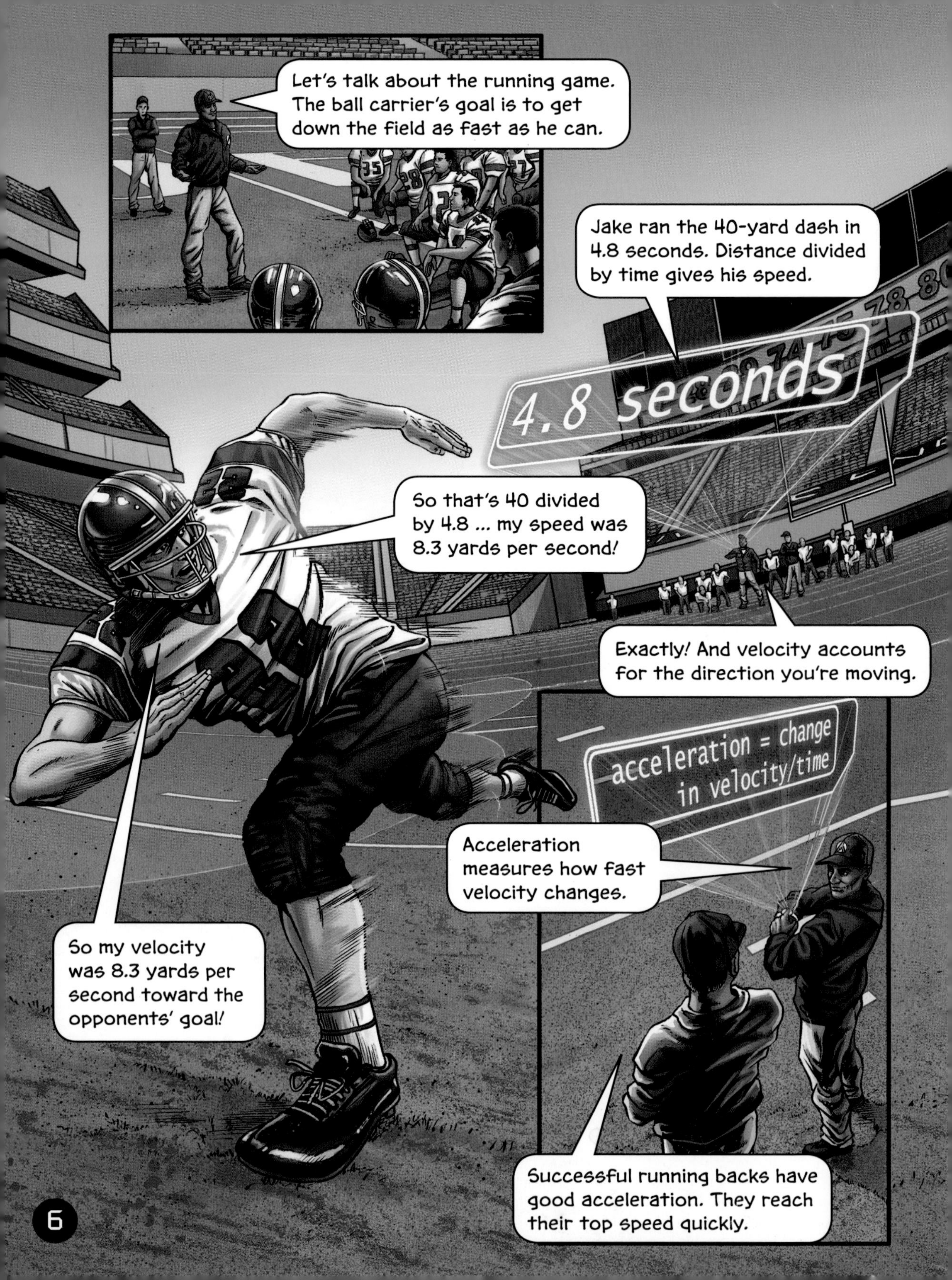
Let's talk about the running game. The ball carrier's goal is to get down the field as fast as he can.
Jake ran the 40-yard dash in 4.8 seconds. Distance divided by time gives his speed.
4.8 seconds
So that's 40 divided by 4.8 ... my speed was 8.3 yards per second!
Exactly! And velocity accounts for the direction you're moving.
So my velocity was 8.3 yards per second toward the opponents' goal!
acceleration = change in velocity/time
Acceleration measures how fast velocity changes.
Successful running backs have good acceleration. They reach their top speed quickly.

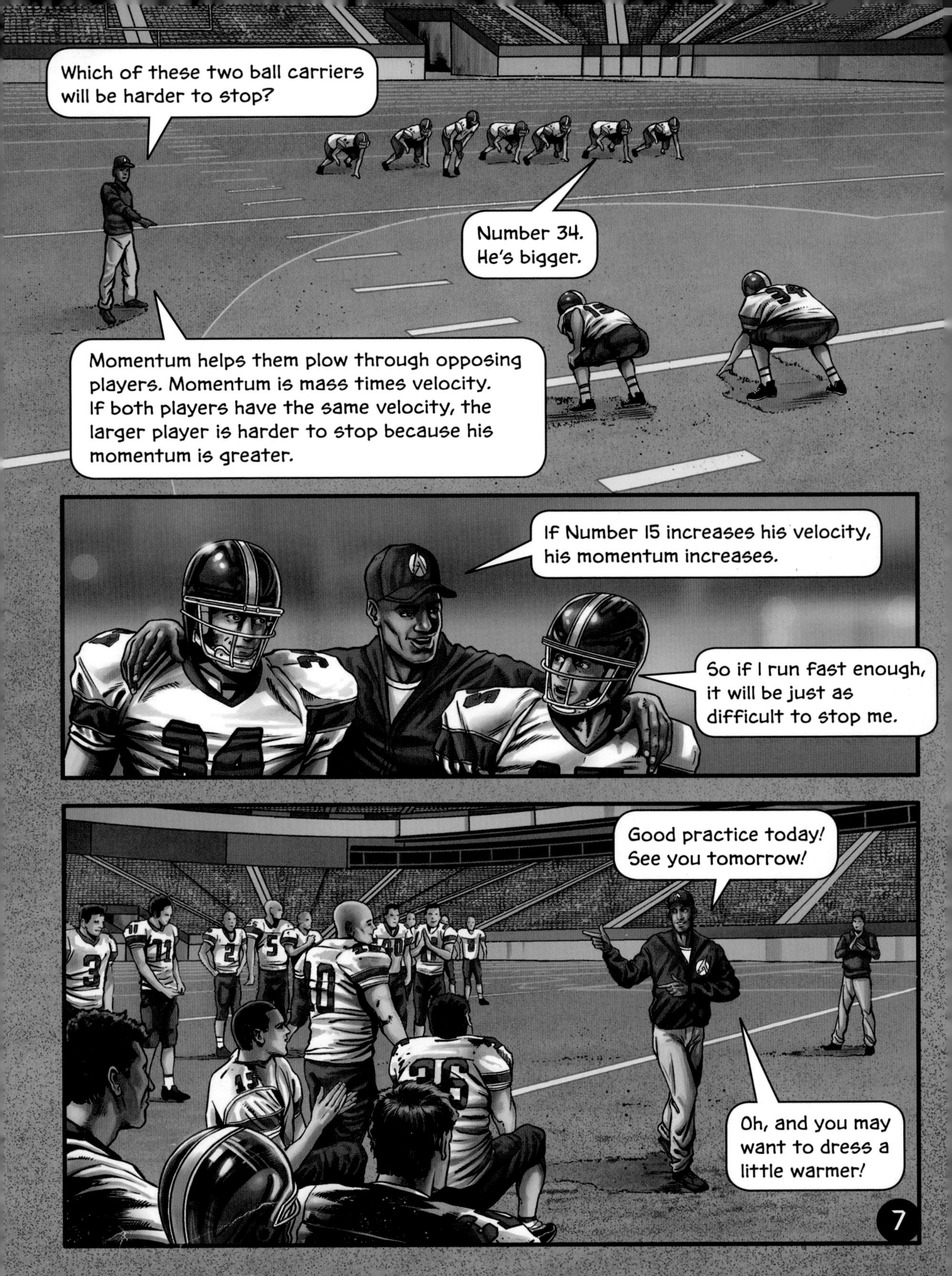
Which of these two ball carriers will be harder to stop?
Number 34. He's bigger.
Momentum helps them plow through opposing players. Momentum is mass times velocity. If both players have the same velocity, the larger player is harder to stop because his momentum is greater.
If Number 15 increases his velocity, his momentum increases.
So if I run fast enough, it will be just as difficult to stop me.
Good practice today! See you tomorrow!
Oh, and you may want to dress a little warmer!

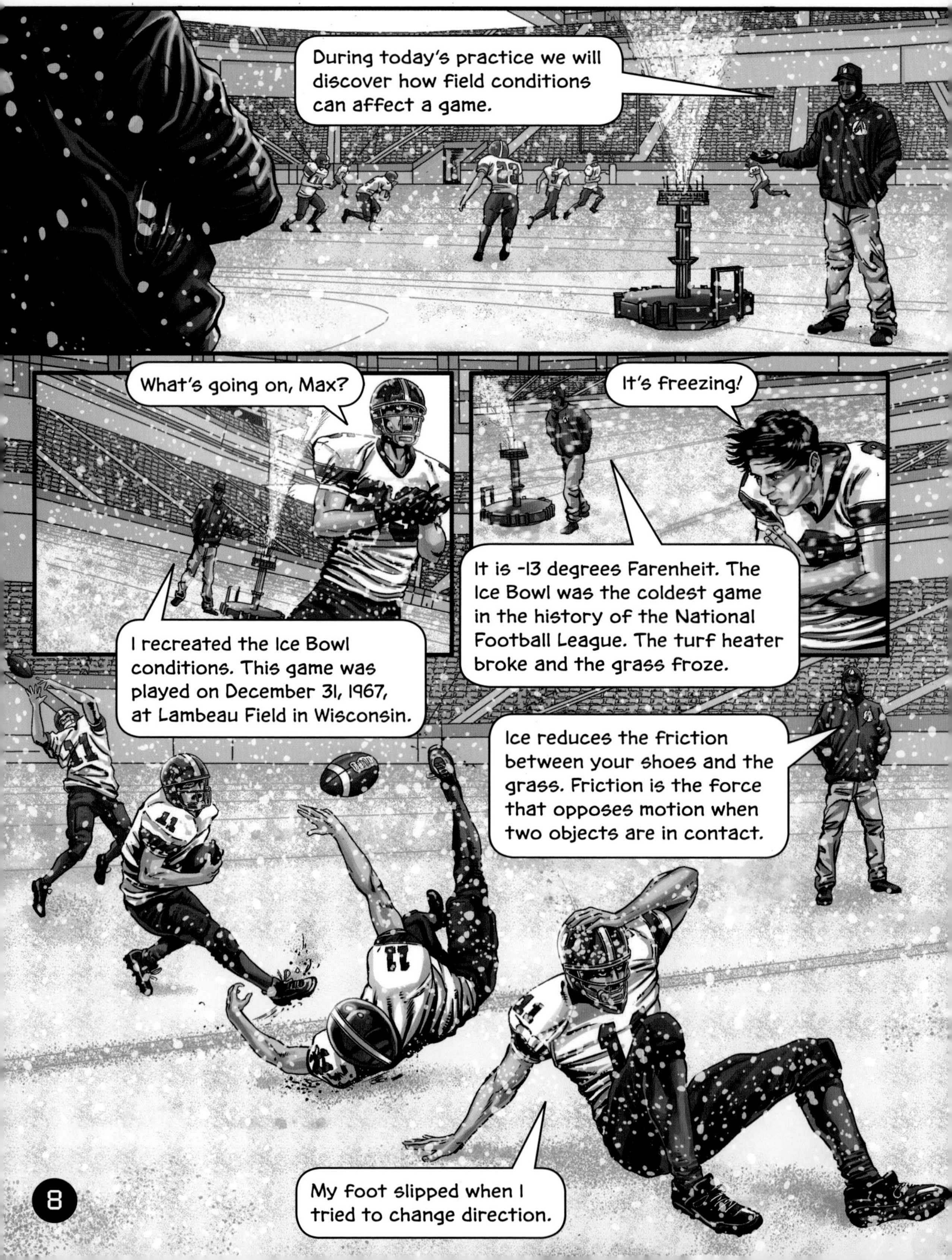
During today's practice we will discover how field conditions can affect a game.
What's going on, Max?
I recreated the Ice Bowl conditions. This game was played on December 31, 1967, at Lambeau Field in Wisconsin.
It's freezing!
It is -13 degrees Farenheit. The Ice Bowl was the coldest game in the history of the National Football League. The turf heater broke and the grass froze.
Ice reduces the friction between your shoes and the grass. Friction is the force that opposes motion when two objects are in contact.
My foot slipped when I tried to change direction.

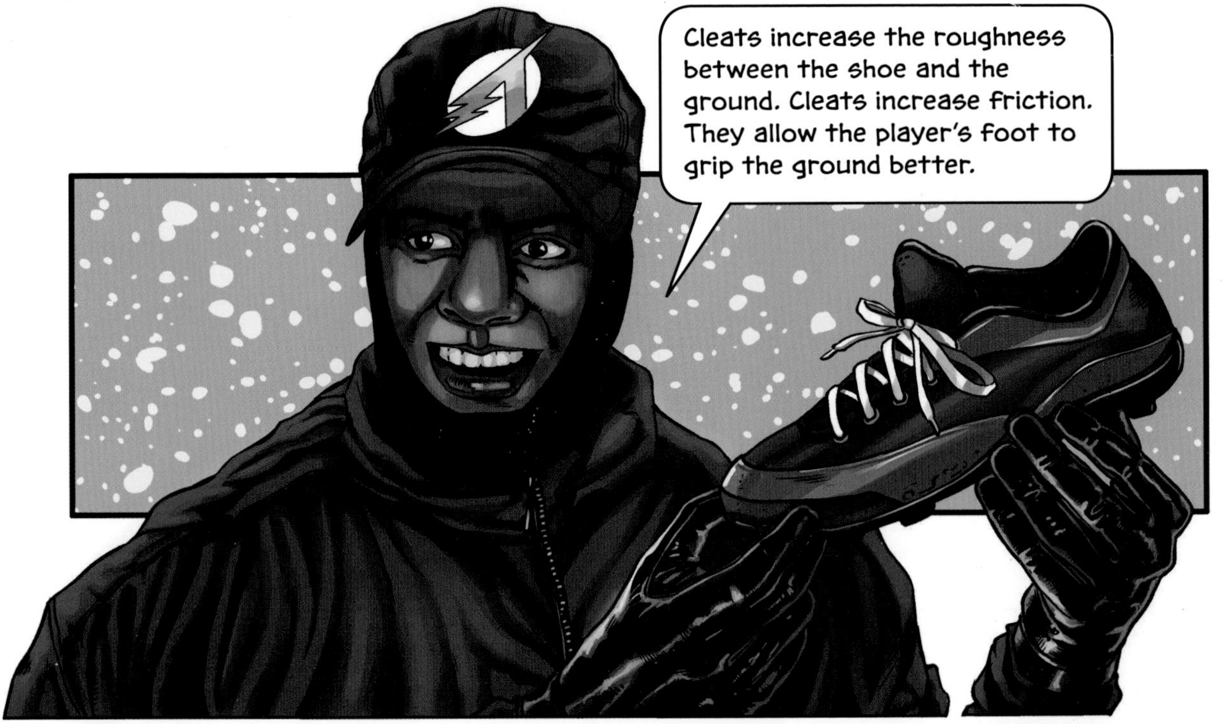
Cleats increase the roughness between the shoe and the ground. Cleats increase friction. They allow the player's foot to grip the ground better.

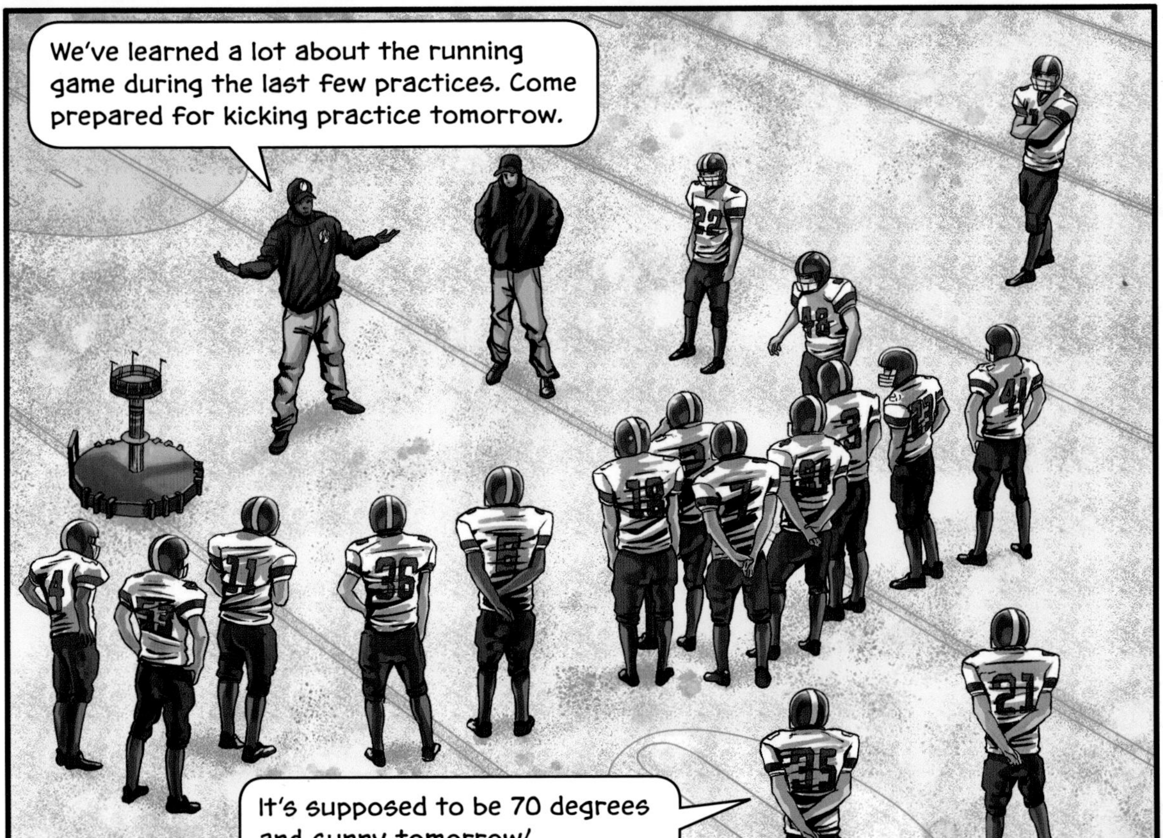
We've learned a lot about the running game during the last few practices. Come prepared for kicking practice tomorrow.
It's supposed to be 70 degrees and sunny tomorrow!

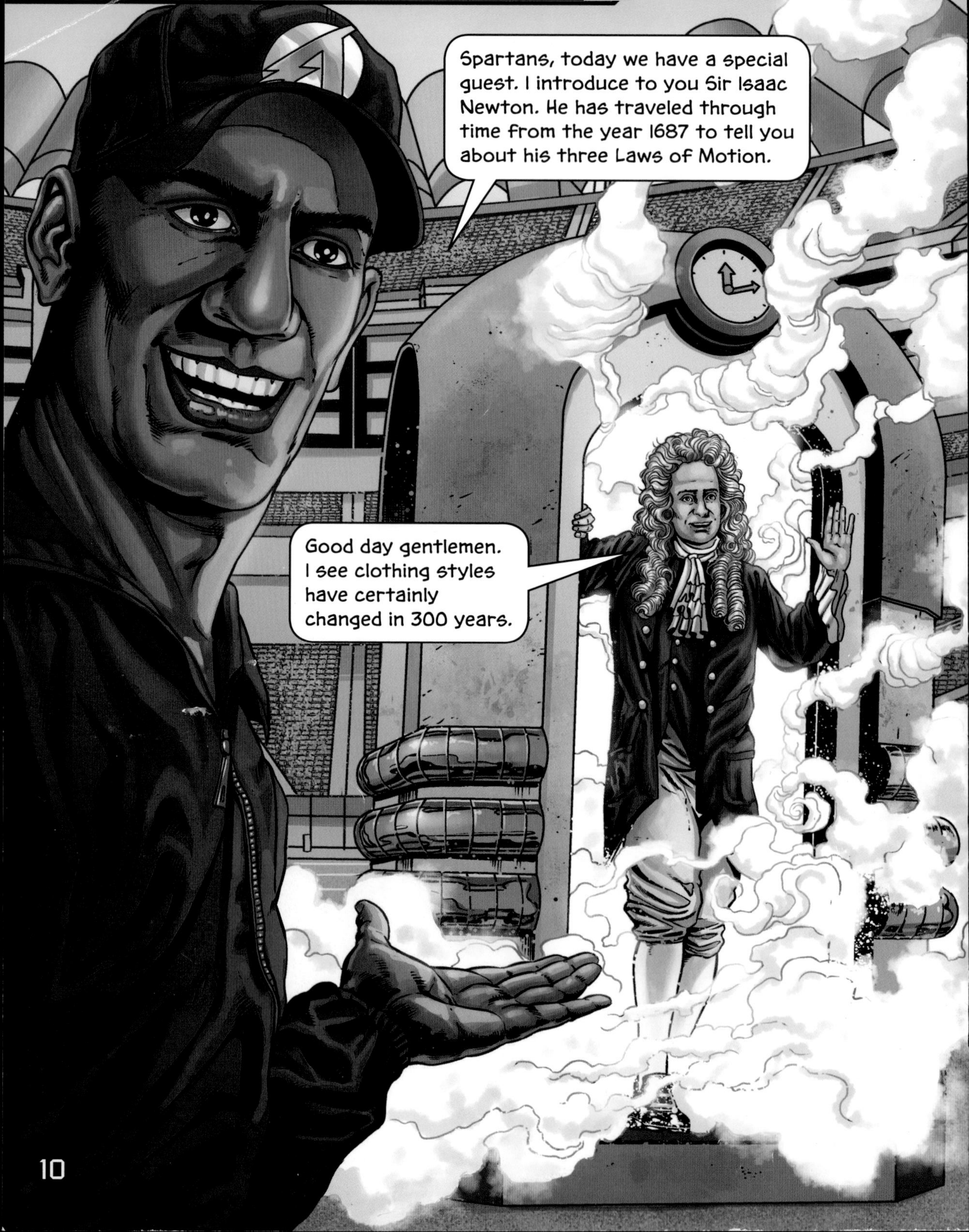
Spartans, today we have a special guest. I introduce to you Sir Isaac Newton. He has traveled through time from the year 1687 to tell you about his three Laws of Motion.
Good day gentlemen. I see clothing styles have certainly changed in 300 years.

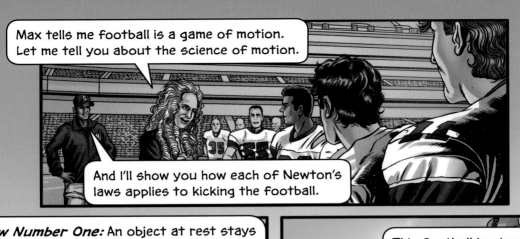

Max tells me football is a game of motion. Let me tell you about the science of motion.

And I'll show you how each of Newton's laws applies to kicking the football.

Law Number One: An object at rest stays at rest, and an object in motion stays in motion, unless a force acts on it.

This football is at rest. According to Newton's First Law, it will remain at rest until I kick it.

But once the football is kicked, it doesn't stay in motion as the law says. It falls back to the ground.

That's because a force acts on it. That force is gravity. It pulls the ball back to the ground.

Isaac Newton was born December 25, 1642, in England. Stories say that he was able to describe gravity after seeing an apple fall to the ground. He concluded that the same force pulling the apple downward also holds the moon in orbit around Earth.

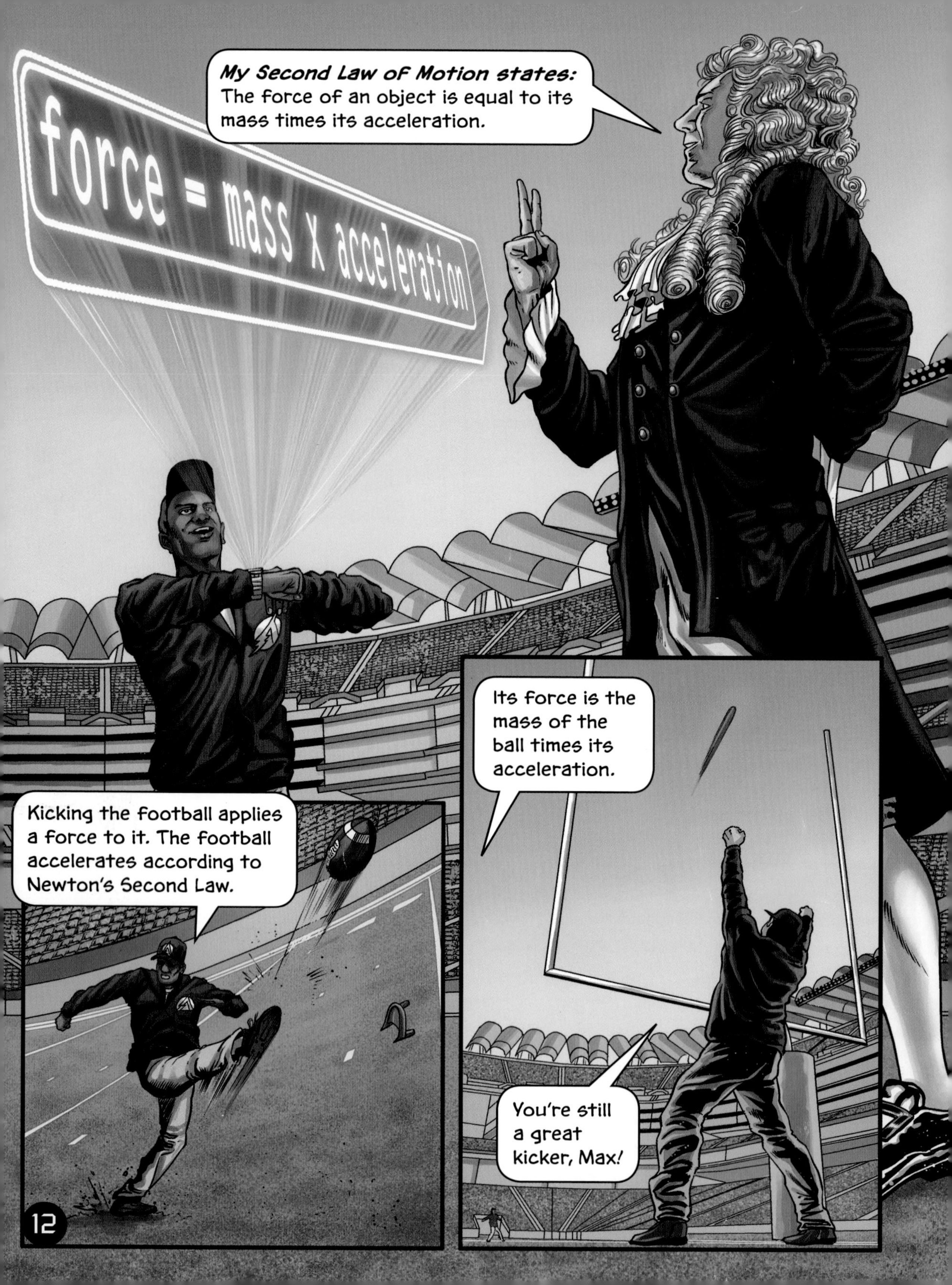
force = mass x acceleration
My Second Law of Motion states: The force of an object is equal to its mass times its acceleration.
Kicking the football applies a force to it. The football accelerates according to Newton's Second Law.
Its force is the mass of the ball times its acceleration.
You're still a great kicker, Max!

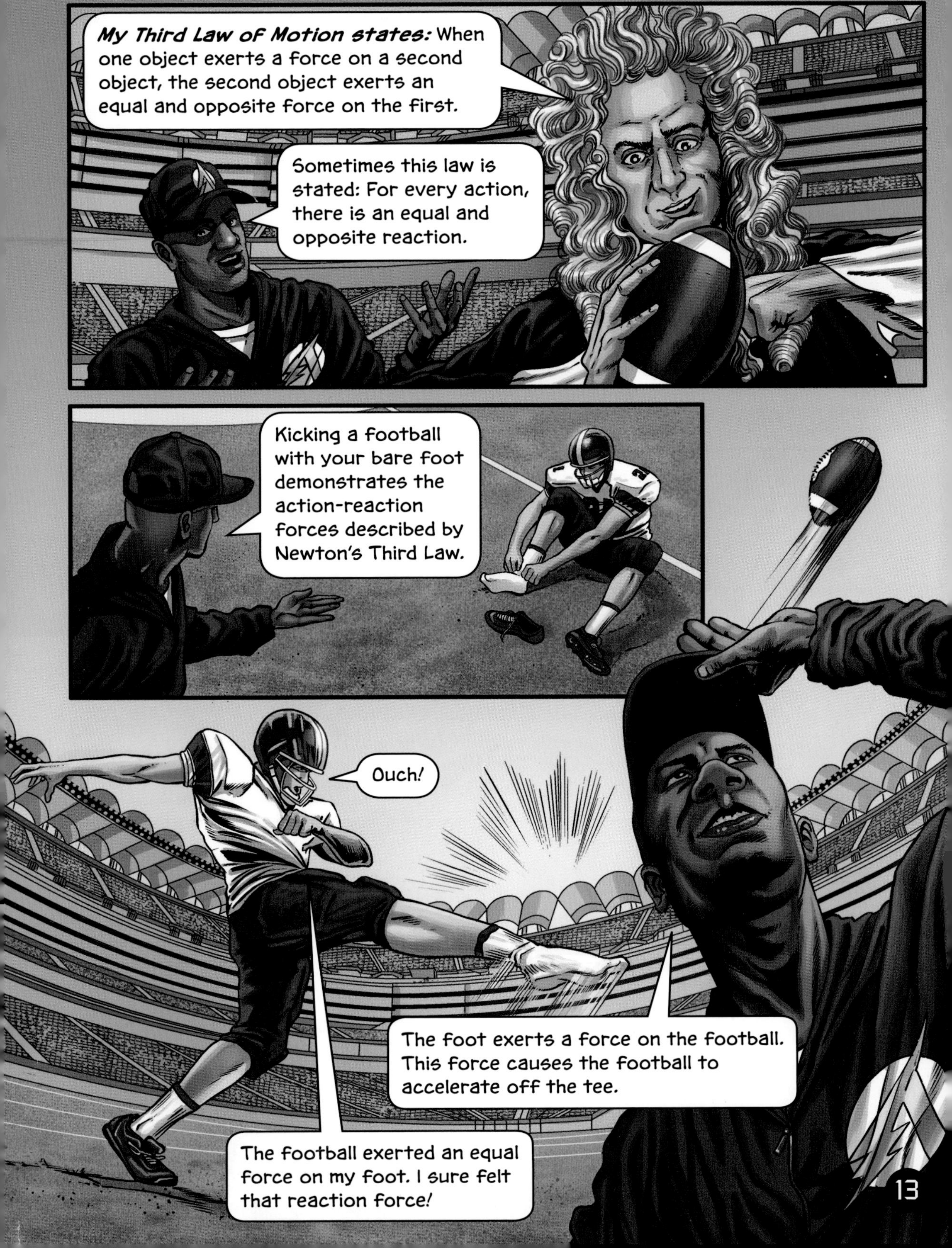
My Third Law of Motion states: When one object exerts a force on a second object, the second object exerts an equal and opposite force on the first.
Sometimes this law is stated: For every action, there is an equal and opposite reaction.
Kicking a football with your bare foot demonstrates the action-reaction forces described by Newton's Third Law.
Ouch!
The foot exerts a force on the football. This force causes the football to accelerate off the tee.
The football exerted an equal force on my foot. I sure felt that reaction force!

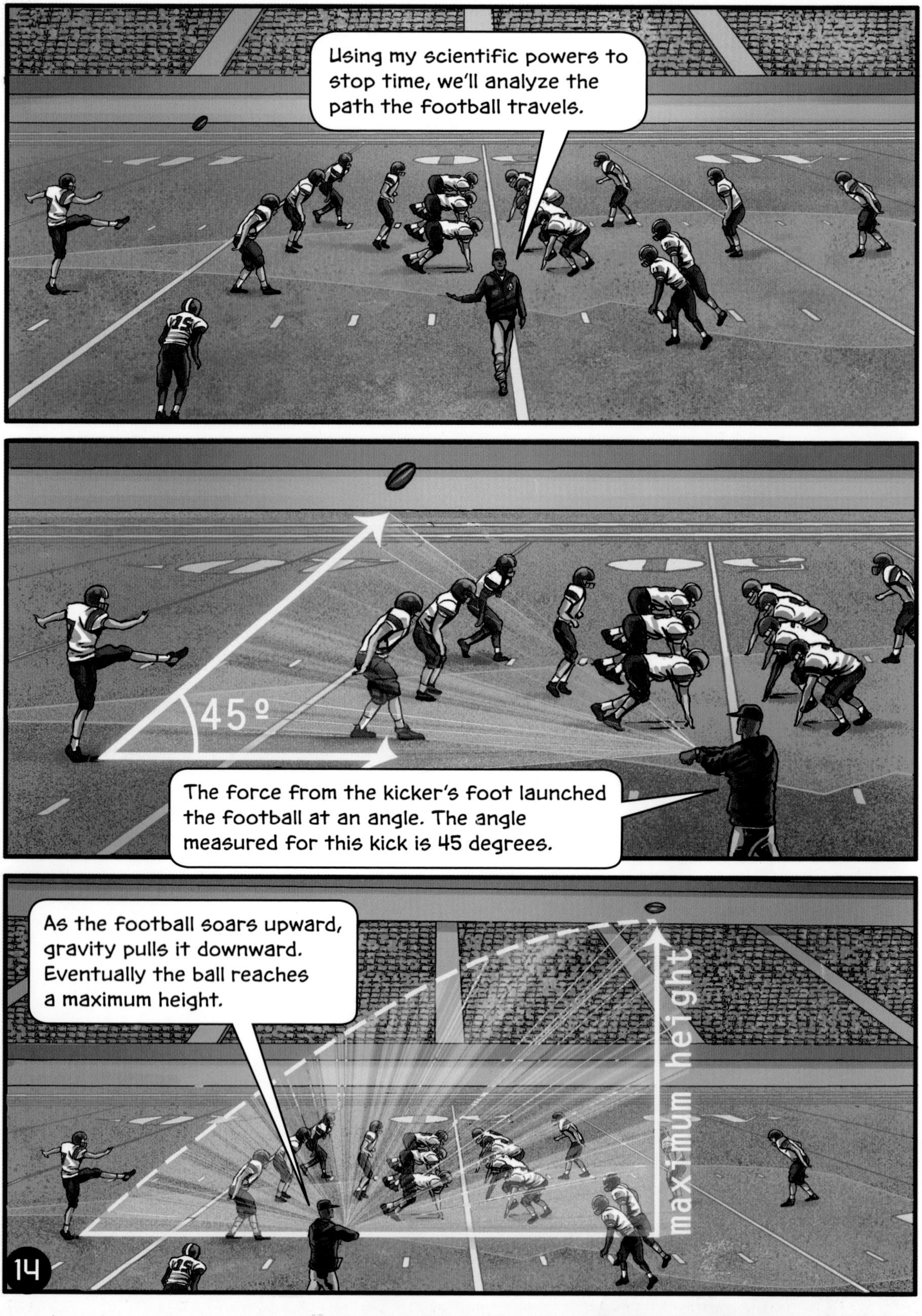
Using my scientific powers to stop time, we'll analyze the path the football travels.
45º
The force from the kicker's foot launched the football at an angle. The angle measured for this kick is 45 degrees.
As the football soars upward, gravity pulls it downward. Eventually the ball reaches a maximum height.
maximum height

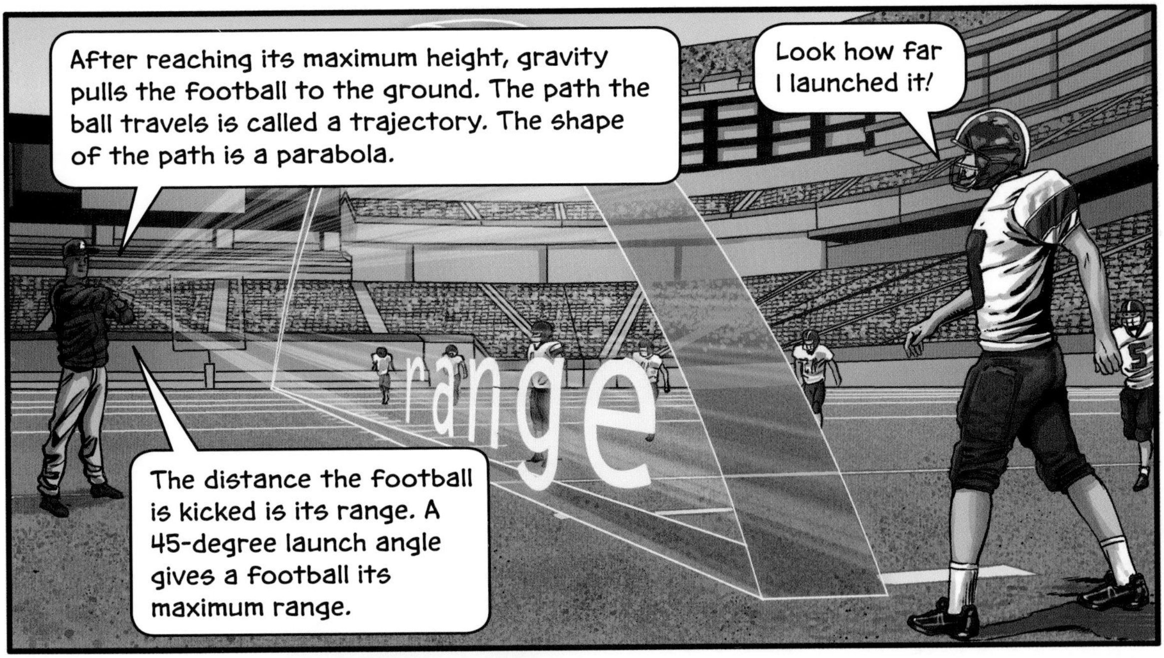
After reaching its maximum height, gravity pulls the football to the ground. The path the ball travels is called a trajectory. The shape of the path is a parabola.
Look how far I launched it!
range
The distance the football is kicked is its range. A 45-degree launch angle gives a football its maximum range.

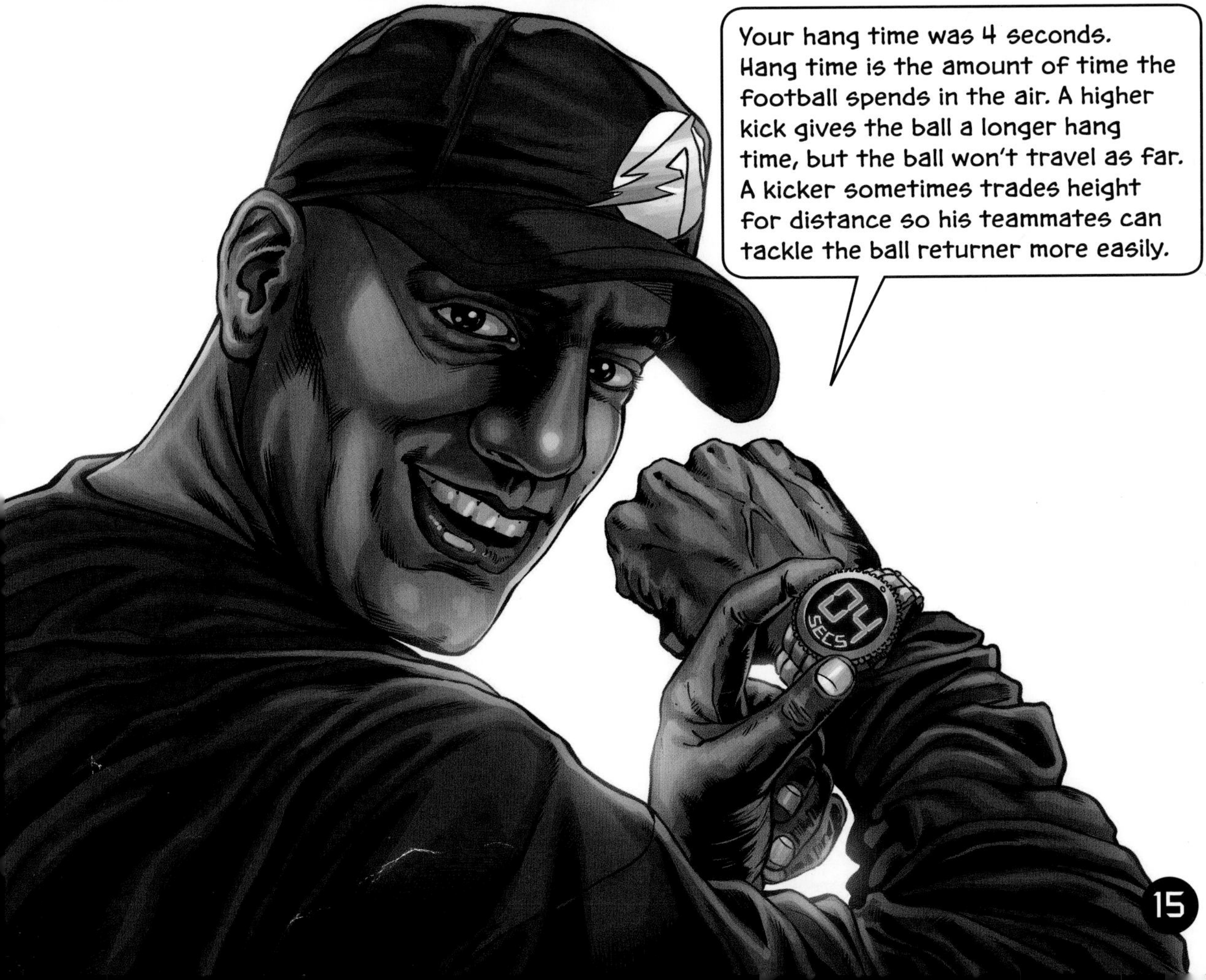
Your hang time was 4 seconds. Hang time is the amount of time the football spends in the air. A higher kick gives the ball a longer hang time, but the ball won't travel as far. A kicker sometimes trades height for distance so his teammates can tackle the ball returner more easily.
04
SECS

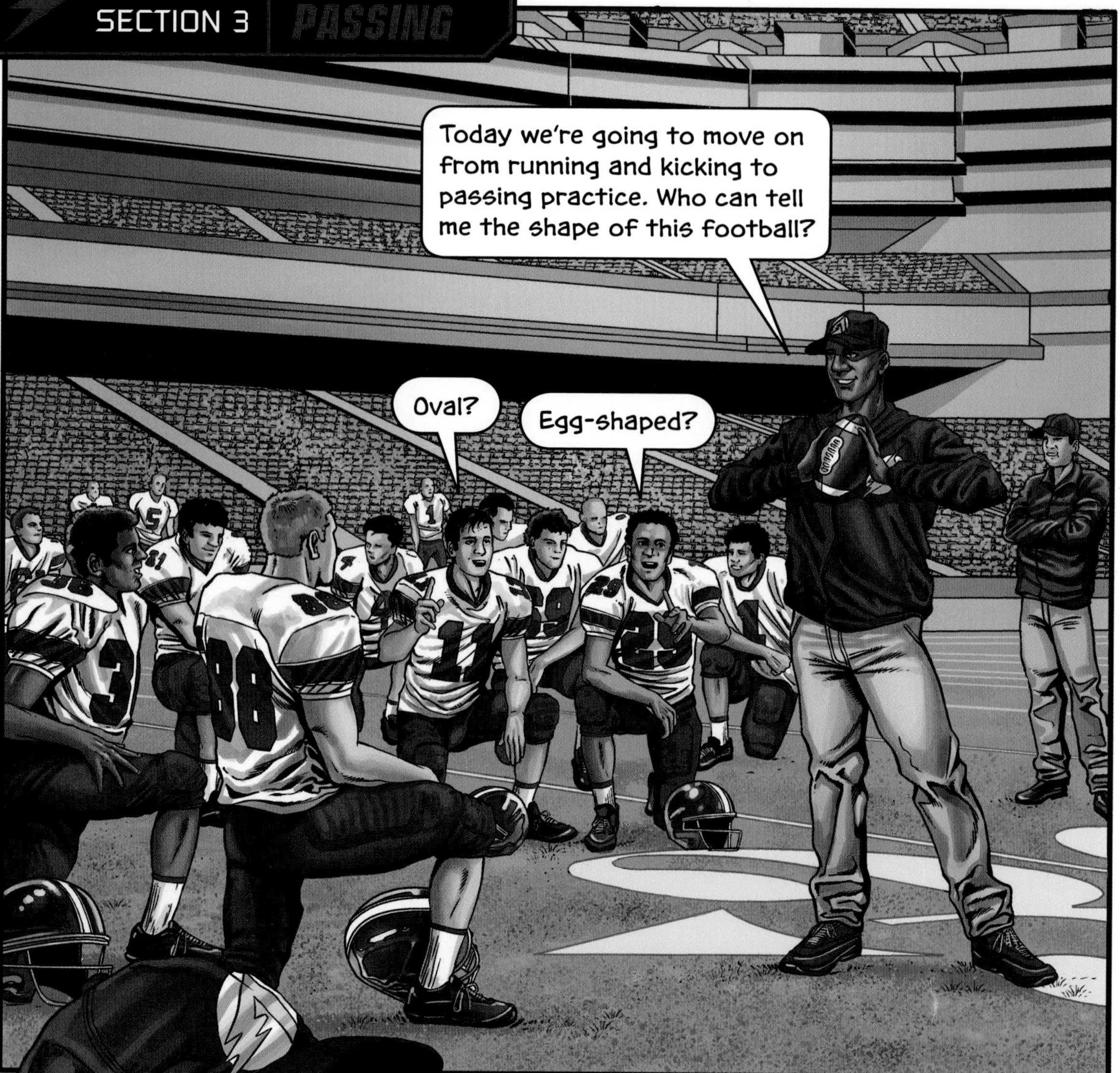
Today we're going to move on from running and kicking to passing practice. Who can tell me the shape of this football?
Oval?
Egg-shaped?

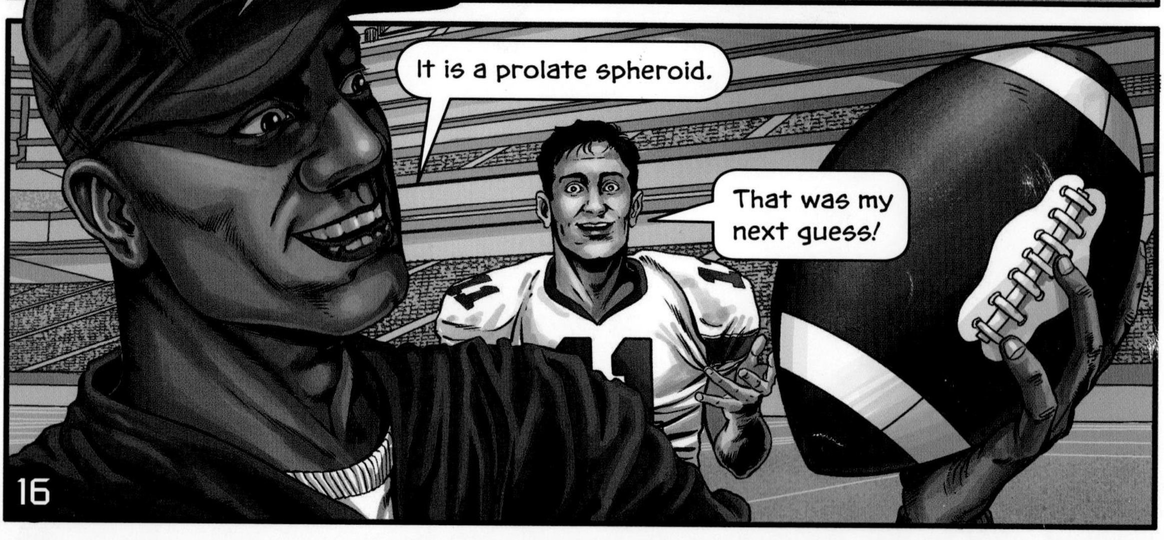
It is a prolate spheroid.
That was my next guess!

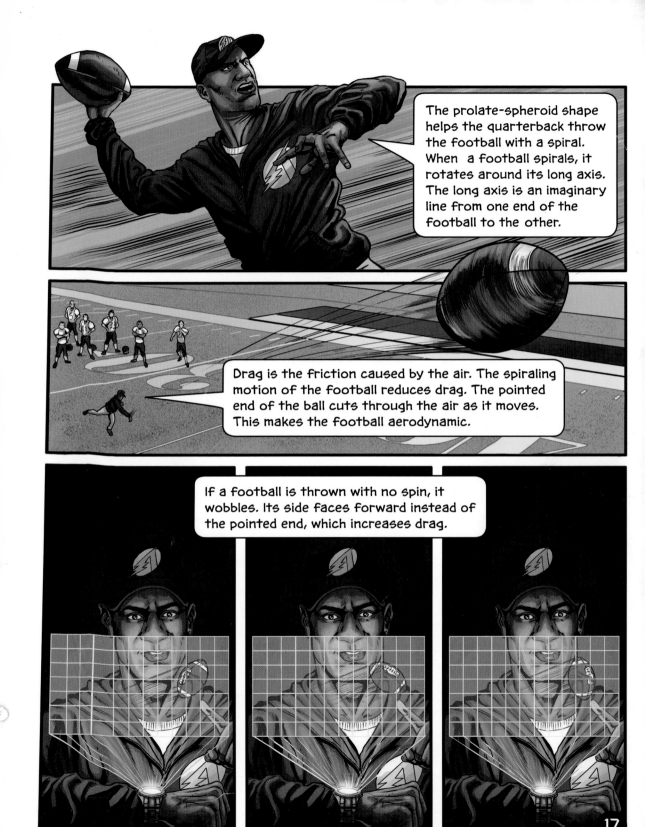

The prolate-spheroid shape helps the quarterback throw the football with a spiral. When a football spirals, it rotates around its long axis. The long axis is an imaginary line from one end of the football to the other.

Drag is the friction caused by the air. The spiraling motion of the football reduces drag. The pointed end of the ball cuts through the air as it moves. This makes the football aerodynamic.

If a football is thrown with no spin, it wobbles. Its side faces forward instead of the pointed end, which increases drag.

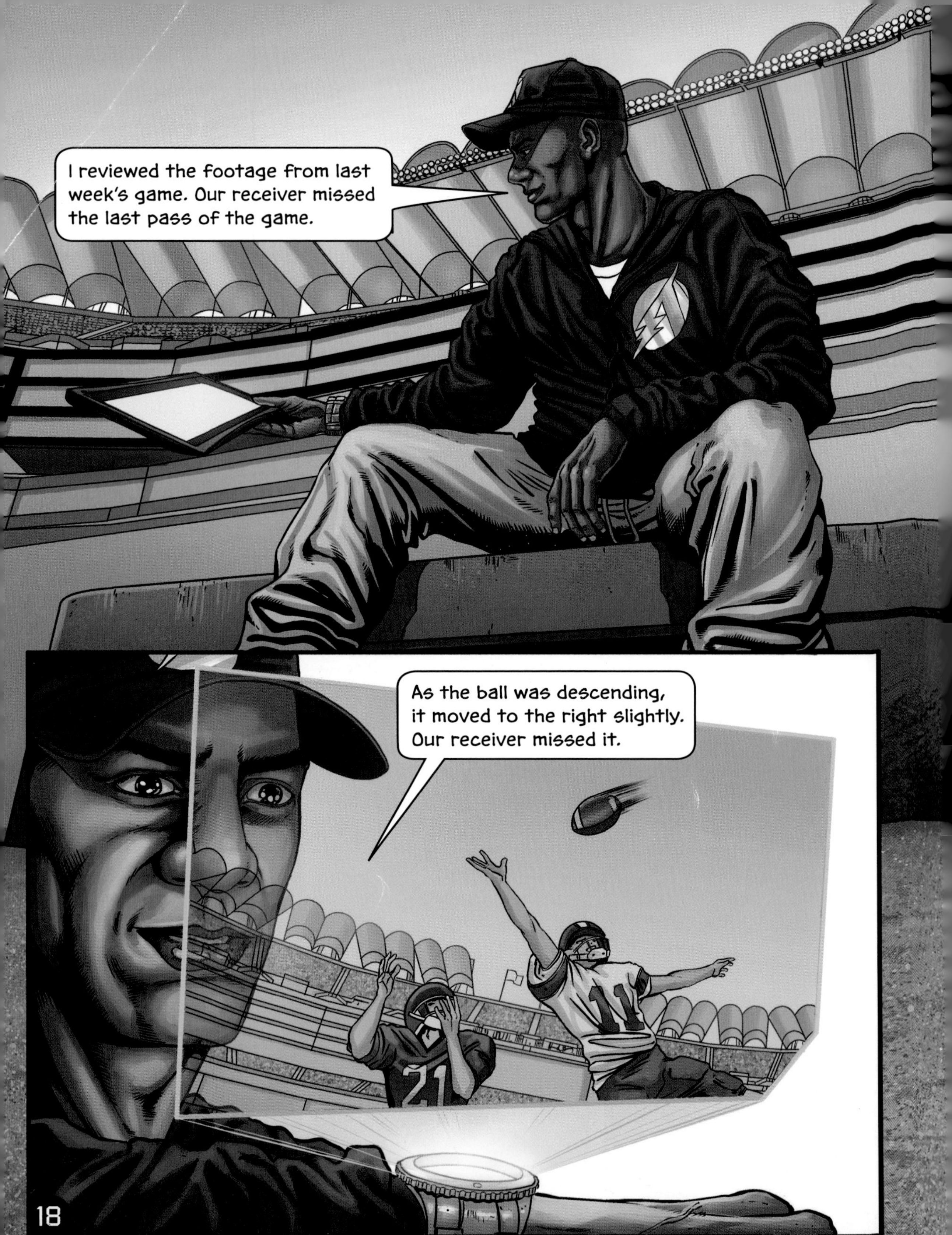
I reviewed the footage from last week's game. Our receiver missed the last pass of the game.
As the ball was descending, it moved to the right slightly. Our receiver missed it.
11
21

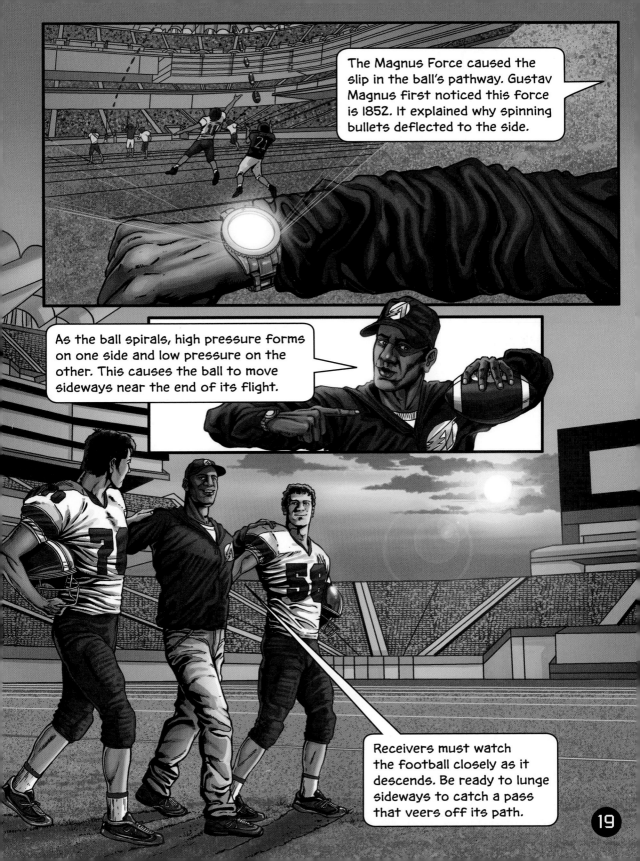

The Magnus Force caused the slip in the ball's pathway. Gustav Magnus first noticed this force is 1852. It explained why spinning bullets deflected to the side.

As the ball spirals, high pressure forms on one side and low pressure on the other. This causes the ball to move sideways near the end of its flight.

Receivers must watch the football closely as it descends. Be ready to lunge sideways to catch a pass that veers off its path.

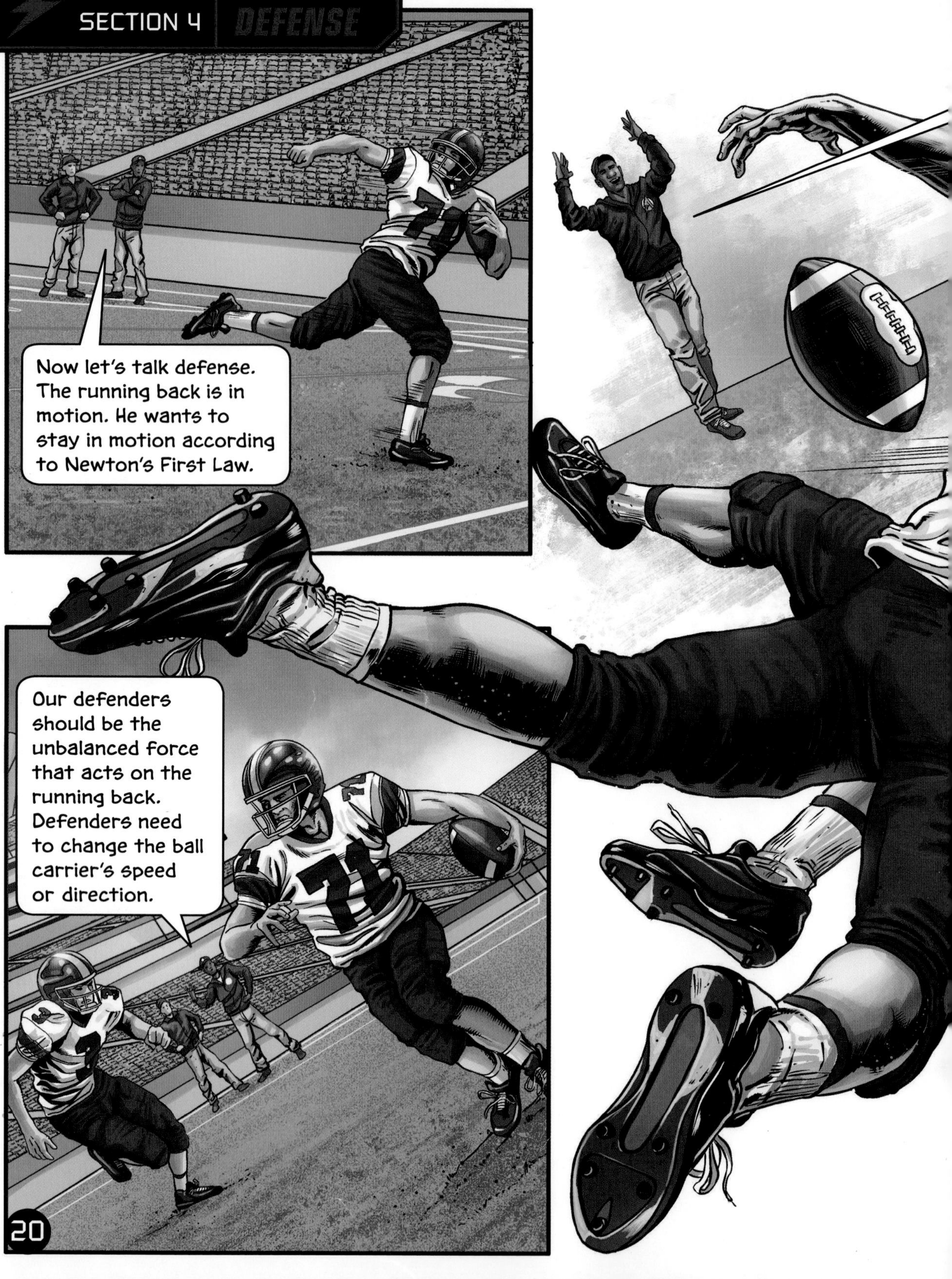
Now let's talk defense. The running back is in motion. He wants to stay in motion according to Newton's First Law.
Our defenders should be the unbalanced force that acts on the running back. Defenders need to change the ball carrier's speed or direction.

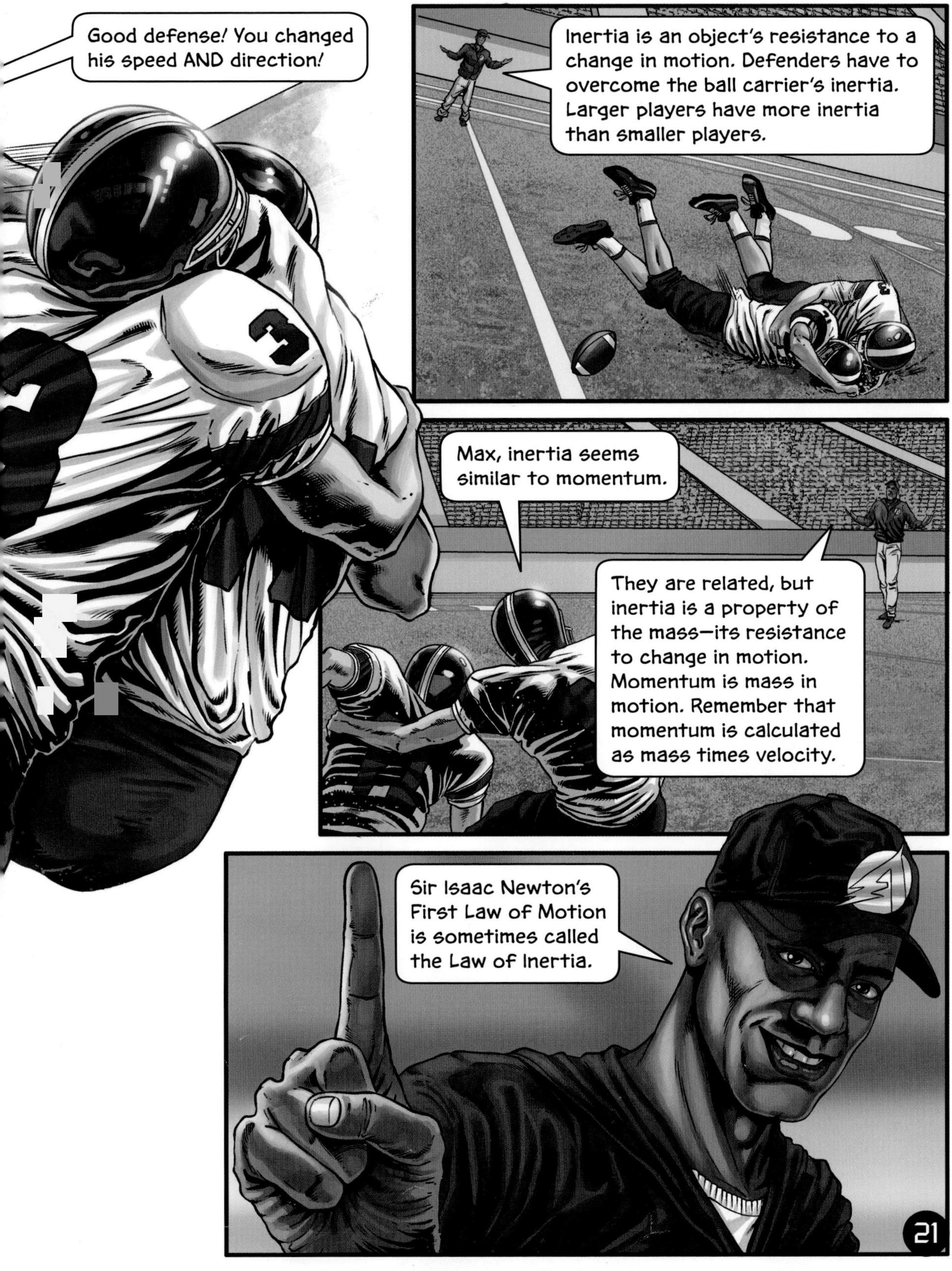
Good defense! You changed his speed AND direction!
Inertia is an object's resistance to a change in motion. Defenders have to overcome the ball carrier's inertia. Larger players have more inertia than smaller players.
3
Max, inertia seems similar to momentum.
They are related, but inertia is a property of the mass—its resistance to change in motion. Momentum is mass in motion. Remember that momentum is calculated as mass times velocity.
Sir Isaac Newton's First Law of Motion is sometimes called the Law of Inertia.

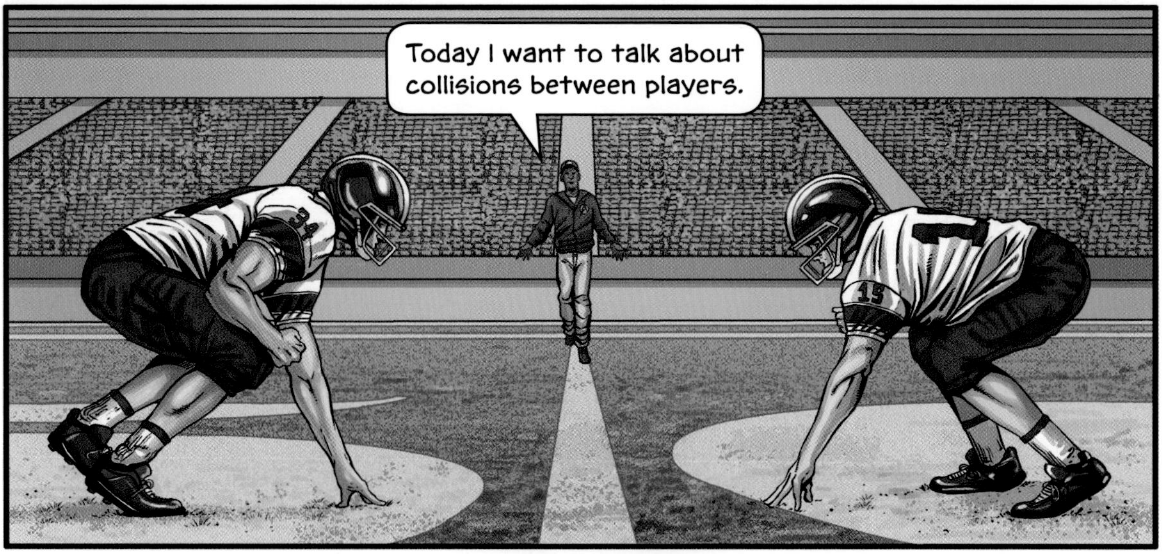
Today I want to talk about collisions between players.

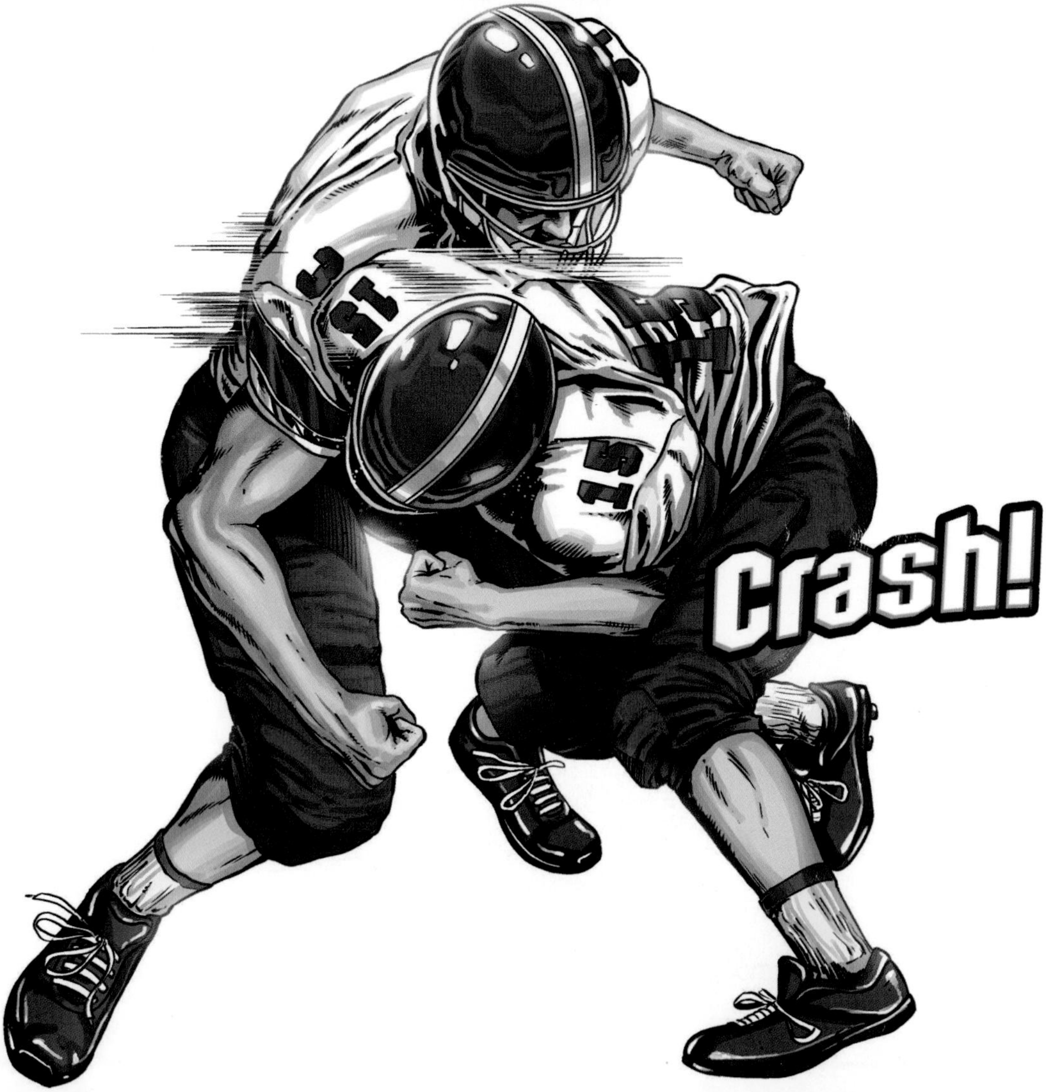
Crash!

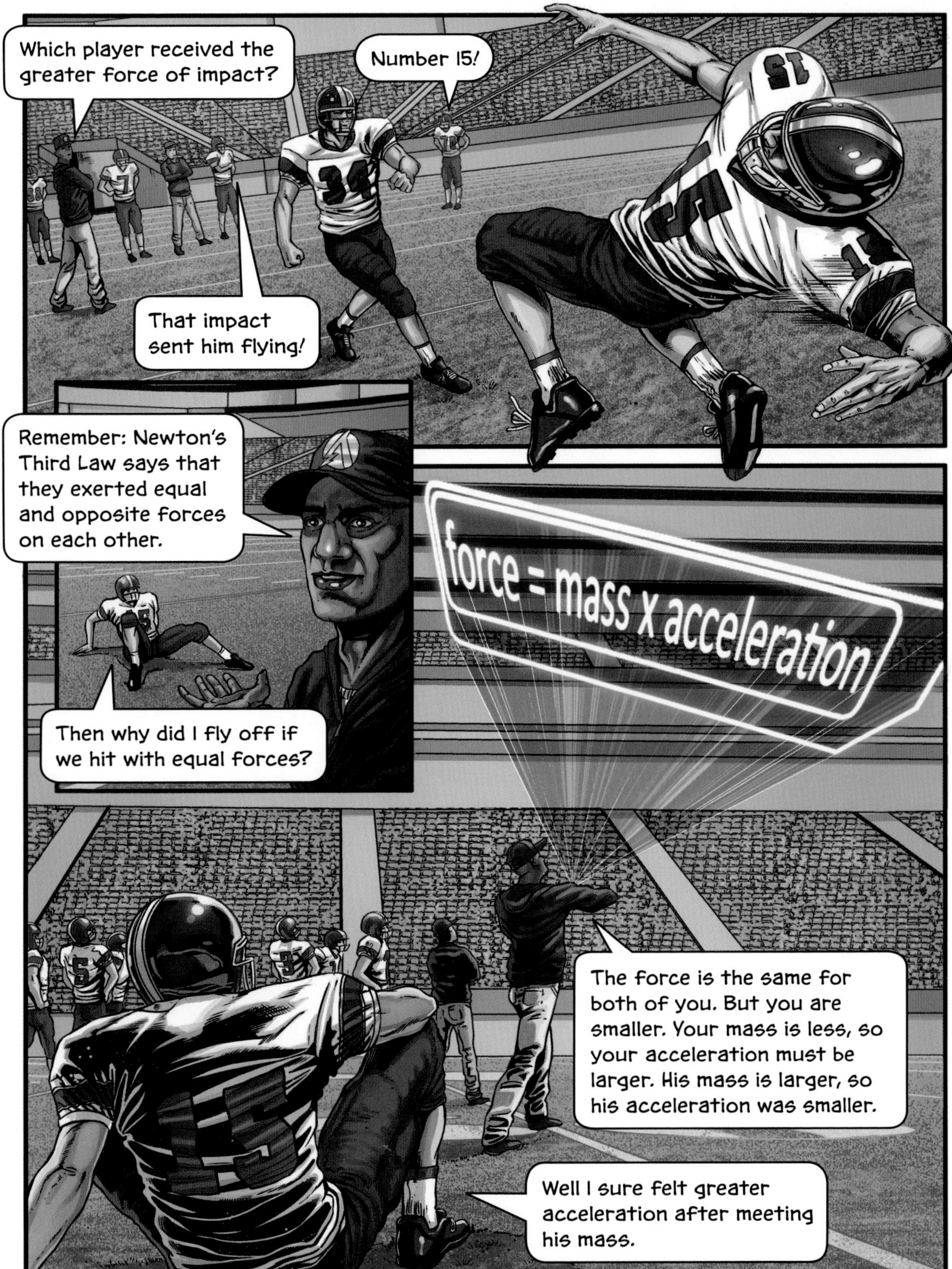
Which player received the greater force of impact?
Number 15!
That impact sent him flying!
Remember: Newton's Third Law says that they exerted equal and opposite forces on each other.
Then why did I fly off if we hit with equal forces?
force = mass x acceleration
The force is the same for both of you. But you are smaller. Your mass is less, so your acceleration must be larger. His mass is larger, so his acceleration was smaller.
Well I sure felt greater acceleration after meeting his mass.

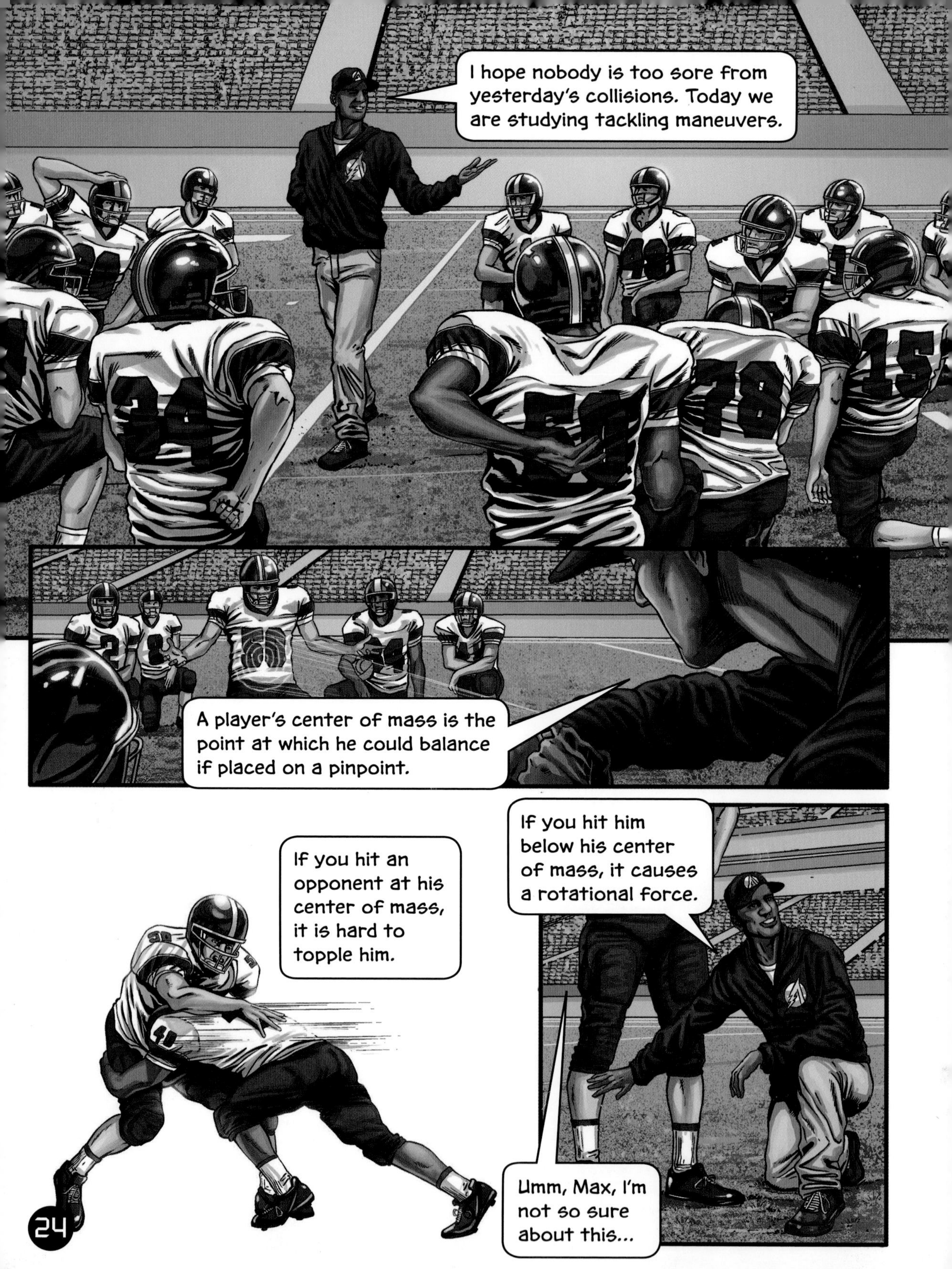
I hope nobody is too sore from yesterday's collisions. Today we are studying tackling maneuvers.
A player's center of mass is the point at which he could balance if placed on a pinpoint.
If you hit an opponent at his center of mass, it is hard to topple him.
If you hit him below his center of mass, it causes a rotational force.
Umm, Max, I'm not so sure about this...

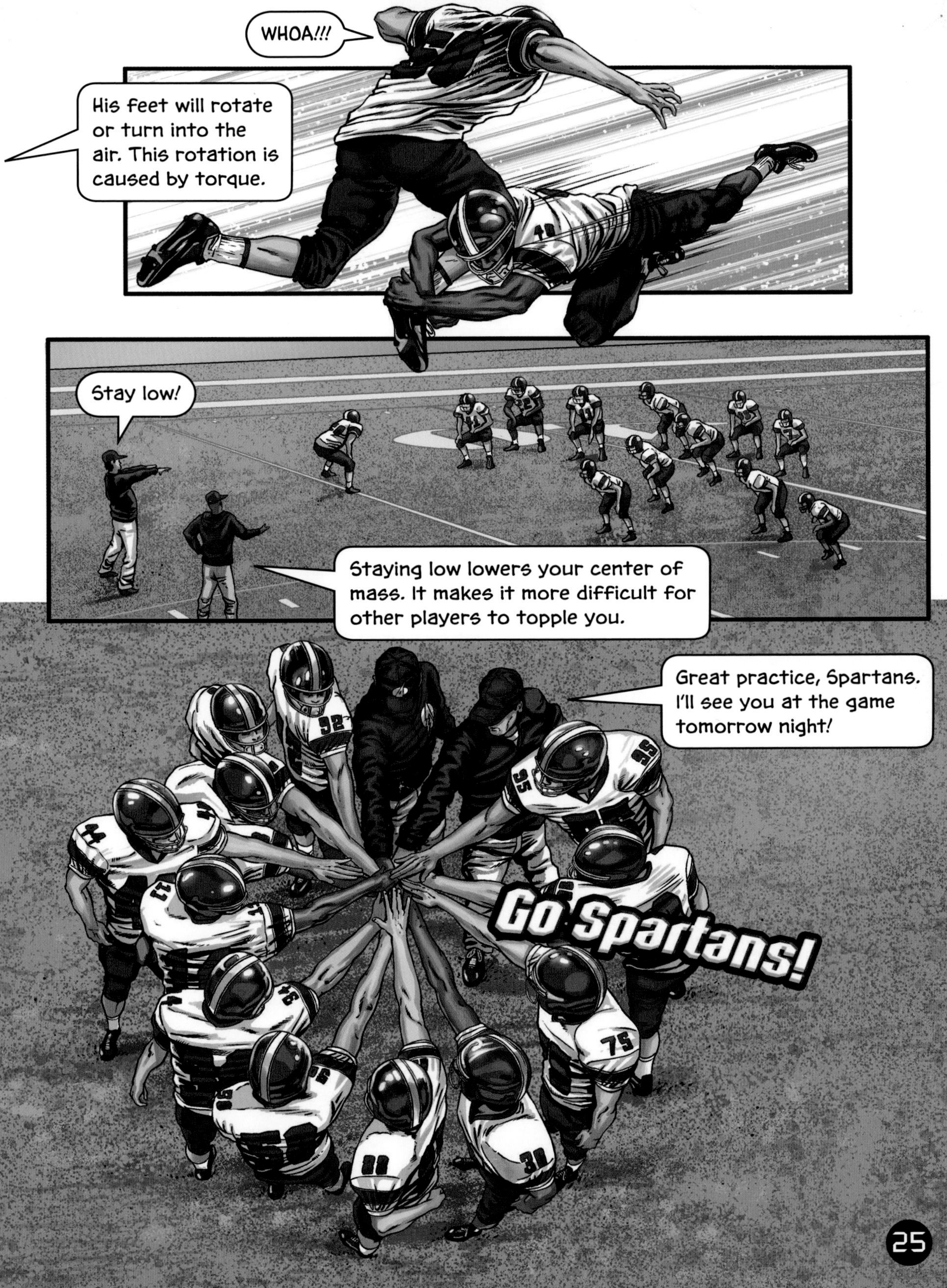
WHOA!!!
His feet will rotate or turn into the air. This rotation is caused by torque.
Stay low!
Staying low lowers your center of mass. It makes it more difficult for other players to topple you.
Great practice, Spartans. I'll see you at the game tomorrow night!
Go Spartans!

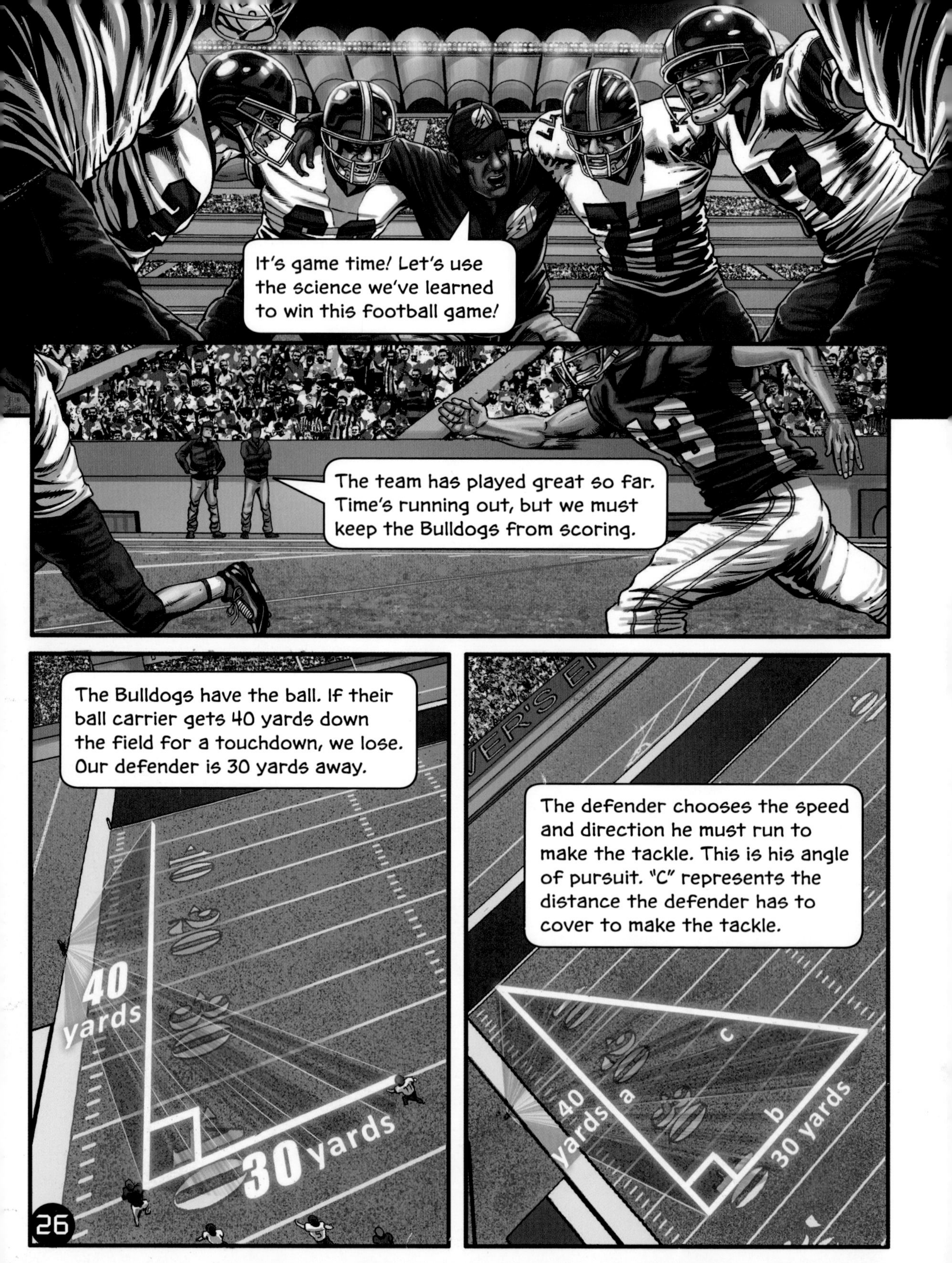

It's game time! Let's use the science we've learned to win this football game!
The team has played great so far. Time's running out, but we must keep the Bulldogs from scoring.
The Bulldogs have the ball. If their ball carrier gets 40 yards down the field for a touchdown, we lose. Our defender is 30 yards away.
40 yards
30 yards
The defender chooses the speed and direction he must run to make the tackle. This is his angle of pursuit. "C" represents the distance the defender has to cover to make the tackle.
c
a
b
40 yards
30 yards

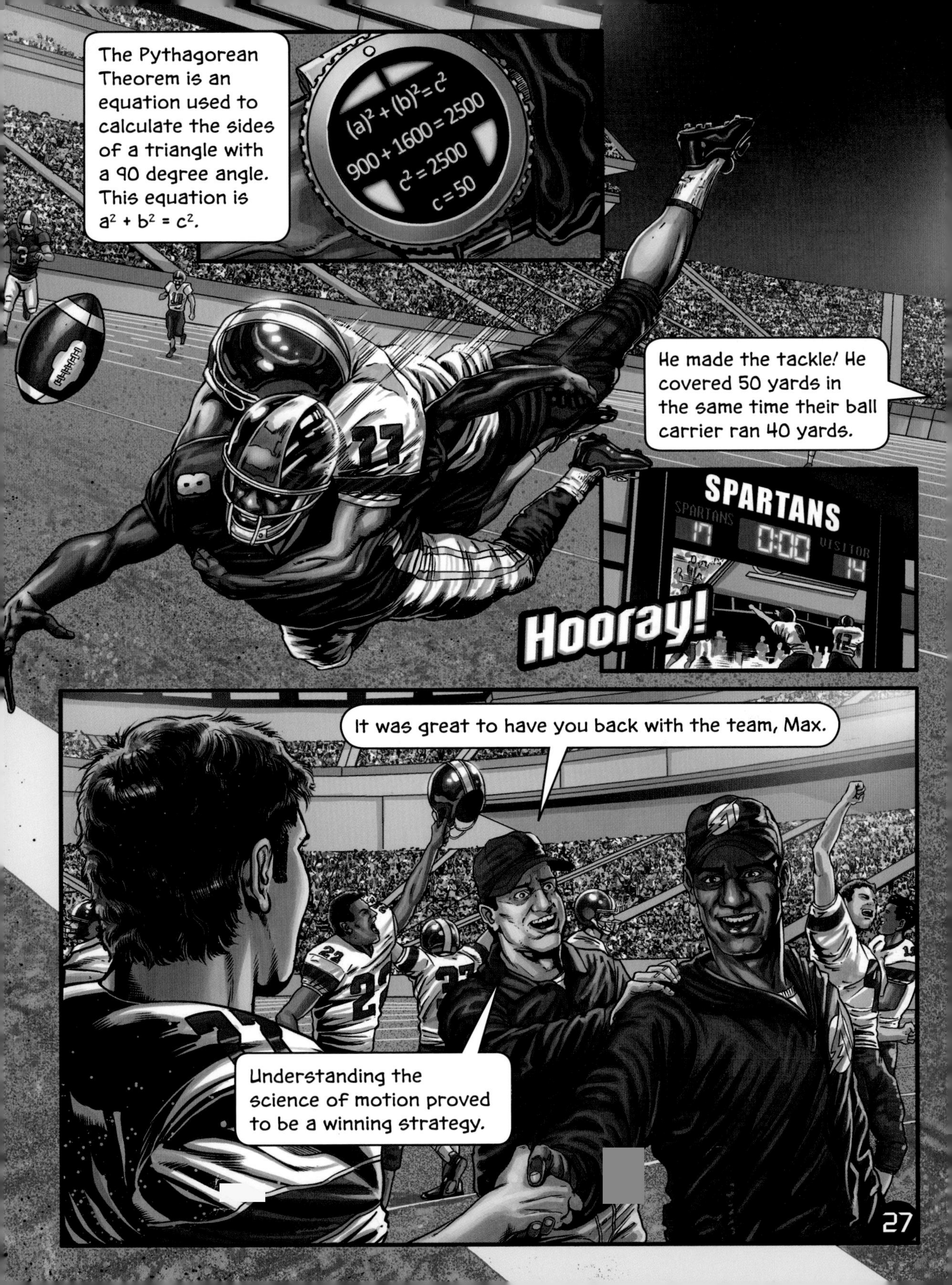
The Pythagorean Theorem is an equation used to calculate the sides of a triangle with a 90 degree angle. This equation is $a^2 + b^2 = c^2$.
$(a)^2 + (b)^2 = c^2$
$900 + 1600 = 2500$
$c^2 = 2500$
$c = 50$
He made the tackle! He covered 50 yards in the same time their ball carrier ran 40 yards.
SPARTANS
SPARTANS 17 0:00 VISITOR 14
Hooray!
It was great to have you back with the team, Max.
Understanding the science of motion proved to be a winning strategy.

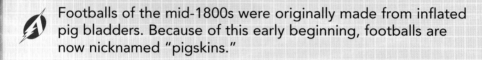

MORE ABOUT FOOTBALL

Footballs of the mid-1800s were originally made from inflated pig bladders. Because of this early beginning, footballs are now nicknamed "pigskins."

The first college football game was played on November 6, 1869, between Rutgers and Princeton. At that time the rules of the game resembled rugby more than modern football.

William "Pudge" Heffelfinger is considered to be the first professional football player. On November 12, 1892, he was paid $500 to play for the Alleghany Athletic Association. Heffelfinger returned a fumble for a touchdown. His team won 4-0. In 1892 touchdowns were only worth 4 points.

Newspapers reported 19 football-related deaths in 1905. President Theodore Roosevelt founded the Intercollegiate Athletic Association of the United States, an early version of today's National Collegiate Athletic Association (NCAA). The Association reformed football rules to make the game safer for the 1906 season.

Football helmets in the early 1900s were made of leather. The first plastic helmets were developed in 1939. The National Football League (NFL) required players to wear helmets beginning in 1943.

Artificial turf was introduced in the Houston Astrodome in the mid-1960s. Artificial turf is made of plastics and nylon. It replaced the grass, which is difficult to grow in a dome with limited sunlight.

In men, the center of mass is located slightly below the belly button. When a football player crouches down, he lowers his center of mass. This makes it more difficult for his opponents to topple him.

 Wireless communication devices have been allowed inside NFL players' helmets. This allows fans watching at home to hear what their favorite players are saying during the game.

 Football exerts a lot of wear and tear on its players and its gear. An NFL team typically goes through about 2,500 pairs of shoes in one season.

MORE ABOUT

SUPER SCIENTIST

Real name: Maxwell J. Axiom
Hometown: Seattle, Washington
Height: 6' 1"   Weight: 192 lbs
Eyes: Brown   Hair: None

Super capabilities: Super intelligence; able to shrink to the size of an atom; sunglasses give x-ray vision; lab coat allows for travel through time and space.

Origin: Since birth, Max Axiom seemed destined for greatness. His mother, a marine biologist, taught her son about the mysteries of the sea. His father, a nuclear physicist and volunteer park ranger, schooled Max on the wonders of earth and sky.

One day on a wilderness hike, a megacharged lightning bolt struck Max with blinding fury. When he awoke, Max discovered a newfound energy and set out to learn as much about science as possible. He traveled the globe earning degrees in every aspect of the field. Upon his return, he was ready to share his knowledge and new identity with the world. He had become Max Axiom, Super Scientist.

GLOSSARY

acceleration (ak-sel-uh-RAY-shuhn)—the change in speed of a moving body

aerodynamic (ayr-oh-dy-NA-mik)—designed to reduce air resistance

drag (DRAG)—the force that resists the motion of an object moving through the air

force (FORSS)—any action that changes the movement of an object

friction (FRIK-shuhn)—a force created when two objects rub together; friction slows down objects

hang time (HANG TYME)—the amount of time the ball spends in the air

inertia (in-UR-shuh)—the tendency of an object to remain either at rest or in motion unless affected by an outside force

mass (MASS)—the amount of material in an object

momentum (moh-MEN-tuhm)—the mass of an object times its velocity; determines how difficult an object is to stop

range (RANJ)—the distance something travels

speed (SPEED)—how fast something moves; speed is a measure of the time it takes something to cover a certain distance

torque (TORK)—the force that causes rotation around an axis

velocity (vuh-LOSS-uh-tee)—the measure of speed and direction something is traveling

READ MORE

McKerley, Jennifer Guess. *Football.* Science Behind Sports. Detroit: Lucent Books, 2012.

Nagelhout, Ryan. *The Science of Football.* Sports Science. New York: PowerKids Press, 2015.

Royston, Angela. *Win That Sprint!: Forces in Sport.* Feel the Force. Chicago: Capstone Heinemann Library, 2015.

Yomtov, Nel. *The Science of a Spiral.* Full-Speed Sports. Ann Arbor, Mich.: Cherry Lake Publishing, 2015.

INTERNET SITES

FactHound offers a safe, fun way to find Internet sites related to this book. All sites on FactHound have been researched by our staff.

Here's all you do:

Visit *www.facthound.com*

Type in this code: 9781491460856

INDEX